STEP-UP
HISTORY

Robert Bruce

Rhona Dick

Evans

Published by Evans Brothers Limited
2A Portman Mansions
Chiltern Street
London W1U 6NR

© Evans Brothers Limited 2006

Produced for Evans Brothers Limited by
White-Thomson Publishing Ltd,
Bridgewater Business Centre,
210 High Street,
Lewes, East Sussex BN7 2NH

Printed in China by New Era Printing Co. Ltd .

Project manager: Ruth Nason

Designer: Helen Nelson, Jet the Dog

Consultant: Dr Raymond McCluskey, Faculty of
Education, University of Glasgow

British Library Cataloguing in Publication Data
Dick, Rhona
    Robert Bruce - (Step-up history)
    1.Robert I, King of Scots, 1274-1329 -
    Juvenile literature
    2. Scotland - Kings and rulers - Biography -
    Juvenile literature
    3. Scotland - History - Robert I, 1306-1929
    I. Title
    941.1'02'092
ISBN-10: 0 237 53096 1
13-digit ISBN (from I Jan 2007) 978 0 237 53096
9

Picture acknowledgements:
Bridgeman Art Library: pages 5t (British Library,
London), 8 (Lambeth Palace Library, London), 12 (©
Glasgow University Library), 14 (Private collection),
21t (Private collection), 24 (Biblioteca Monasterio
del Escorial, Madrid, Giraudon); Corbis: pages 9b
(Angelo Hornak), 16 (Homer Sykes), 25bl
(McPherson Colin/Corbis Sygma), 26 (Polak
Matthew/Corbis Sygma); Rhona Dick: page 22;
Mary Evans Picture Library: pages 5b, 23; Doug
Houghton Photography: pages 10b, 17b; Helen
Nelson: pages 1, 6, 9t, 25t, 25br, 27r; Science
Photo Library: page 27l (Michael Donne, University
of Manchester); SCRAN: pages 5c (Private coll-
ection), 10t (James Gardiner), 11 (Stirling Smith Art
Gallery and Museum), 15t (National Trust for
Scotland), 15b (National Trust for Scotland), 17t
(West of Scotland Archaeology Service), 18
(National Trust for Scotland), 19 (National
Museums of Scotland); Topfoto: page 21b.

Maps and battle plans by Helen Nelson.

Also available: *Step-up Geography: Scotland*
Further titles relating to Scotland in preparation:
Step-up History: Mary Queen of Scots
Step-up History: Famous Scots

Contents

The two kingdoms

Scotland and England at war ...

For centuries Scotland had its own monarch and, in 1139, King Stephen of England signed a treaty stating that Scotland was an independent country. Yet there were often disputes between the neighbouring kingdoms of Scotland and England. The borderlands became a battleground for Scottish and English armies, each trying to gain more territory. After some battles, Scottish kings were forced to pay homage to English monarchs.

... and at peace

The two countries were not always at war and there were some close links between their ruling families. For example, before he became king of Scotland in 1124, David I lived in England and became a friend of the English king, Henry II. He introduced some of Henry's ideas about monarchy to Scotland. Later Alexander III (1249-86) married Margaret, the daughter of the English king Henry III.

The close relationships between the Scottish and English monarchs ensured that there was peace between the two countries until the end of the 13th century. Alexander III of Scotland and Edward I of England were brothers-in-law. They had great respect for each other. Find them on the timeline below.

▼ *This timeline shows the rulers of Scotland and England in the 13th and 14th centuries. Between 1290 and 1292 and between 1296 and 1306 there was no ruler in Scotland.*

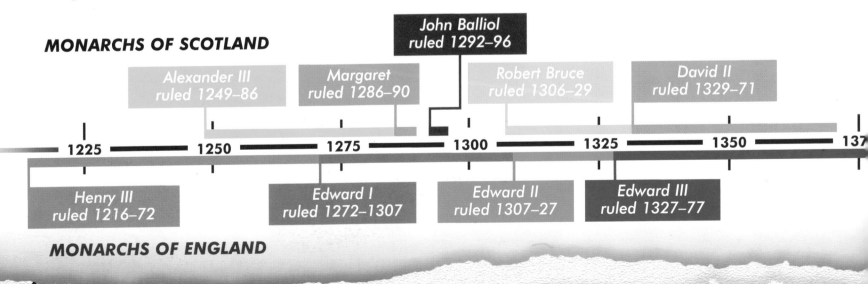

MONARCHS OF SCOTLAND

John Balliol
ruled 1292–96

Alexander III
ruled 1249–86

Margaret
ruled 1286–90

Robert Bruce
ruled 1306–29

David II
ruled 1329–71

1225 1250 1275 1300 1325 1350 137

Henry III
ruled 1216–72

Edward I
ruled 1272–1307

Edward II
ruled 1307–27

Edward III
ruled 1327–77

MONARCHS OF ENGLAND

Edward I's wars in Wales

Edward I became king of England in 1272. He was very ambitious, wanting to enlarge his kingdom and become a more powerful ruler. In 1276 he invaded Wales and for the next eight years his army was busy fighting the Welsh. Edward I built many strong castles in Wales to demonstrate his power and to control the Welsh people.

◀ *This picture from a 14th-century manuscript shows Edward I making his son, Edward, the Prince of Wales.*

Scotland's fight for independence

Perhaps Edward I's successes in Wales encouraged him to think that he could be king of Scotland too. In this book you will find out what happened when Edward invaded Scotland in 1296. You will meet some of the people who played a major part in Scotland's struggle for independence in the late 13th and early 14th centuries.

◀ *William Wallace is remembered as a hero in the fight for independence. Find out why on page 10. No one knows exactly what people from this time looked like. Artists have put their own interpretation on the characters.*

▶ *This is how one artist pictured Robert Bruce, who became king in 1306. His father and grandfather were also called Robert Bruce. His grandfather is known as Bruce 'the Competitor'.*

A kingdom without a monarch

Alexander III and his wife Queen Margaret had two sons and one daughter, but by 1284 all except the king were dead. Only the daughter, Margaret, who had married King Erik of Norway, had had any children. The Scottish parliament decided that her baby daughter, also named Margaret, was the heir to Alexander's throne.

Alexander believed that Scotland needed a strong monarch to keep the country independent. He married again, hoping to have more sons to be his heirs. Then, one stormy night in March 1286, he set out from Edinburgh to go home to his new queen at Kinghorn in Fife. On the way his horse fell over a cliff. The king was killed.

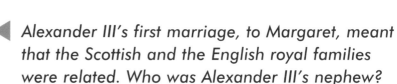

◄ A memorial marks the spot at the foot of the cliff where Alexander III died.

◄ Alexander III's first marriage, to Margaret, meant that the Scottish and the English royal families were related. Who was Alexander III's nephew?

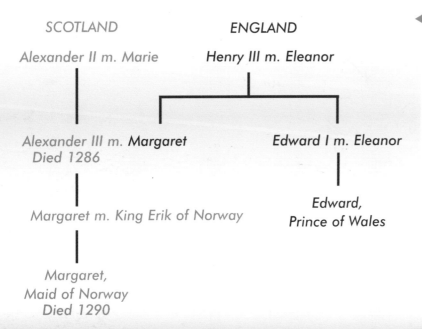

SCOTLAND

Alexander II m. Marie

Alexander III m. Margaret
Died 1286

Margaret m. King Erik of Norway

Margaret,
Maid of Norway
Died 1290

ENGLAND

Henry III m. Eleanor

Edward I m. Eleanor

Edward,
Prince of Wales

The Maid of Norway

Alexander's granddaughter and heir, Margaret, was known as 'the Maid of Norway'. She was aged only three when Alexander died and so six Guardians (two earls, two bishops and two barons) were appointed to rule Scotland in her name, until she was older.

In 1290 Scotland and England signed the Treaty of Birgham. It stated that Margaret, Maid of Norway, would be queen of Scotland and would marry Edward, Prince of Wales – the son of Edward I.

Good or bad?

List (1) the terms of the Treaty that were good for England and (2) the terms that were good for Scotland. Did both countries benefit equally?

The terms of the Treaty of Birgham

- The Maid of Norway will marry Edward, Prince of Wales.
- The laws, liberties and customs of Scotland will be maintained.
- The Great Offices of State will be held by Scotsmen.
- Taxes will only be raised in Scotland for the benefit of Scotland.
- People accused of crimes committed in Scotland must be tried in Scotland.
- The important churchmen in England will not interfere in matters of the church in Scotland.
- No parliament dealing with Scottish affairs will be held outside Scotland.
- No one holding land in Scotland will do homage outside Scotland.
- The Scottish kingdom will be 'separate, apart and free in itself without subject to the English kingdom saving the rights of the king of England'.

The voyage to Scotland

Margaret was a sickly child but, in 1290, aged seven, she was considered old enough to make the long sea journey from Norway to Scotland. Edward I sent a ship for her, supplied with food for the journey, but her father, King Erik, insisted that she should sail in a Norwegian vessel. The voyage was harsh, and Margaret, Maid of Norway and queen of Scotland, died either at sea or in the Orkneys. Her body was buried in Bergen.

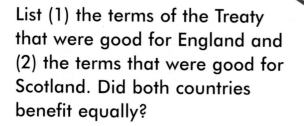

The Maid of Norway sailed from Bergen and should have landed at Leith – a journey, via Orkney, of about 650 miles.

No heir to the throne

Margaret's death caused great concern in Scotland. There was now no direct heir to the throne, and no one to protect the kingdom from its greedy neighbour. Scotland's struggle for independence was about to begin.

The new king of Scotland

After Margaret's death, 13 people, including her father, the king of Norway, claimed the Scottish throne. One of the Guardians wrote to Edward I for advice and so the English king had a chance to interfere in Scottish affairs. He felt that helping to choose Scotland's next king made him more important than that king.

Edward reaches a decision

Eventually there were only two real contenders, John Balliol and Robert Bruce, known as 'the Competitor'. You can see from this family tree that both were descended from David I.

A large group of auditors listened to the arguments and, in November 1292, after more than a year of debate, Edward decided that John Balliol would be king.

King John

John was crowned and swore an oath of loyalty to Edward I as his feudal overlord.

▶ *King John pays homage to Edward I.*

▼ *John Balliol was descended from the older of David I's two great grand-daughters. This made his claim to the throne stronger than that of Bruce 'the Competitor'.*

David I (reigned 1124–53)
|
Henry, Earl of Northumbria

- Malcolm IV (reigned 1153–65)
- William I (reigned 1165–1214)
  |
  Alexander II (reigned 1214–49)
  |
  Alexander III (reigned 1249–86)
- David, Earl of Huntingdon
  - Margaret
    |
    Devorguilla
    - Eleanor
    - John Balliol
  - Isabel
    |
    Robert Bruce 'the Competitor'

The oath meant that King John had to obey Edward, and could not fight against him. Scotland had become an English possession. With no real power, John became known as 'Toom Tabard', which means 'Empty Coat'.

Some nobles supported John, but Bruce 'the Competitor' retired in anger to his lands in southwest Scotland. He swore loyalty to Edward I but never to King John.

From bad to worse

In 1293 Edward I revoked the Treaty of Birgham, which had guaranteed Scottish independence. The next year he insisted that Scotland provide soldiers to help him fight against France.

John Balliol was the last king to be crowned on the Stone of Destiny at Scone. This is a replica of it. Edward I stole the Stone and sent it to England in 1296. It was kept under his throne.

The Scottish nobles were worried that King John would never stand up to Edward I, so they set up a Council of twelve to rule Scotland in his name. They also agreed with France that Scotland and France would support each other in any war against England.

Invasion

In 1296 Edward I invaded Scotland. His army attacked and plundered the rich trading town of Berwick and continued north, defeating the Scots at Dunbar and marching on to Elgin. King John was captured and imprisoned in the Tower of London, England's strongest prison.

Why do you think the Bruce family and some others did not respond when the Council called on Scots to defend their land against Edward?

Find out about John Balliol

Make a table, with the headings shown below. Use it to list five things that you want to find out about John Balliol. Then complete the other two columns.

John Balliol

What I want to find out	Where I might find out	What I found out

William Wallace

The beginnings of unrest

Think what would change for Scots people after Edward revoked the Treaty of Birgham, especially the term about taxes (see page 7). Many people resented the changes and the English invasion of their country.

From 1296 landholders in Scotland were expected to swear an oath of loyalty to Edward I. Some refused, including William Wallace, who took to the forests as an outlaw.

Words for Wallace

Read the story of Wallace on these pages. Then write a list of words to describe him: for example 'patriot', 'brave'. Use the words to help you write a poem telling part of Wallace's story.

Scotland has many memorials to Wallace, including this monument on the Abbey Craig, a hill near the site of the Battle of Stirling Bridge, and this statue in Aberdeen.

Gradually others followed Wallace, to fight the English. However, Scottish nobles did not support Wallace, who was not of noble birth.

Nor did the nobles support Andrew Moray, who led a band of rebel Scots in the northeast. Moray and his men took back land from the English until most of the area north of the River Forth was in Scottish hands. Edward I then sent a large army to Scotland.

IN HONOUR OF
WILLIAM WALLACE
GUARDIAN OF SCOTLAND

The Battle of Stirling Bridge

It seemed that if Edward's army could cross the River Forth at Stirling, its military strength would crush Moray's rebellion. Wallace's men joined forces with Moray's army and they marched south.

On 10 September 1297, Wallace and Moray positioned their army on the Abbey Craig, overlooking the Forth. The next morning they waited until about 5,000 English soldiers had crossed the wooden bridge. Then they ordered their men to rush down the hill and attack. Many English soldiers were savagely slaughtered. Their horses could not manoeuvre properly in the boggy ground and retreat was difficult. When the bridge collapsed, even more English soldiers died by drowning.

Two months after this victory for the Scots, Moray died from his wounds. Wallace was made a Guardian, in the name of King John.

Defeat and the final years

In 1298 Edward turned his attention again to Scotland. At Falkirk, on 22 July, Wallace was defeated by the greater numbers of English soldiers and weaponry. Wallace then resigned as Guardian and went into hiding, spending many years on the Continent of Europe.

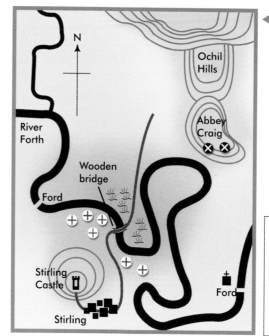

The English had three times as many men as the Scots. But the Scots had an advantage, being up on the Abbey Craig.

⊗	Scots
+	English
⚜	Boggy ground
〃	High ground

▼ *Wallace's careful planning helped to win the Battle of Stirling Bridge, even though the English had better weapons.*

When he returned to Scotland he was betrayed, perhaps by his own servant. He was captured, taken to London and tried for treason. He was executed in a most cruel way on 23 August 1305.

The nobles of Scotland

Feudalism

In the early 12th century, David I had introduced the idea of feudalism to Scotland. It was like a pyramid system with the king at the top, owning all the land.

King

Nobles

Knights

Tenant farmers

At each level, the feudal overlords promised to protect their vassals (the people to whom they leased land), and the vassals agreed to perform military duties. However, in reality, it was rarely as simple as this!

The king leased land to wealthy nobles, who swore an oath of loyalty to him. They also agreed to provide knights and infantry in times of war.

The nobles leased part of their land to knights, and the knights leased some of their land to peasants, who were called 'tenant farmers'.

Peasants like this farmer feeding acorns to his pigs were at the bottom level of the feudal system.

Many powerful noble families owned land both in England and in Scotland. Try to think why this would cause problems, because of the feudal system, when the two countries were at war.

Anglo-Norman castle builders

Some noble families in Scotland, such as the Balliols, the Bruces and the Comyns, were Anglo-Norman. They were descendants of Normans who had arrived in England with William the Conqueror in 1066. They spoke a dialect of French.

When Anglo-Norman noblemen first arrived in Scotland, after about 1124, they thought that they needed to protect themselves from the Scots. Therefore they built castles at sites that could be easily defended – for example, on crags, islands and land partly protected by rivers. At first the castles were simple wooden structures, on top of man-made mounds. Afterwards sturdy stone fortresses were built.

Rival families

As time went on, Anglo-Norman noblemen married Scotswomen, uniting powerful Anglo-Norman and Scottish families. Nevertheless there was often rivalry between families. Some nobles who angered the king had their land confiscated and given to another family. The Comyns supported John Balliol's claim to the throne in 1290, and this

Draw a medieval castle

Visit http://www.castlesontheweb.com/ and use the glossary section to find out what these features of a castle are:
- Motte
- Bailey
- Crenellation
- Donjon
- Fosse
- Curtain wall
- Drawbridge
- Loopholes

Use photos from the website to help you draw a castle and label each feature.

infuriated the Bruces. As king, John Balliol confiscated Bruce lands and gave them to the Comyns. Other families took sides with either the Comyns or the Bruces.

The Wars of Independence

The nobles were also divided in their feelings about Edward I's part in ruling Scotland. The divisions between them made them less likely to succeed in the wars against the English.

Dirleton Castle was captured by the English in 1298. The Anglo-Norman castles were important in the Wars of Independence. They gave English soldiers a stronghold from which to control the surrounding land. If the Scots captured one of the castles they destroyed it. Why do you think they did that?

Robert Bruce becomes king

The Bruce family had always been loyal to Edward I. They were among the nobles who signed the oath of loyalty to Edward in 1296. But in 1297 Robert Bruce, the grandson of Bruce 'the Competitor', changed his mind. He was of royal blood, tracing his ancestors back, like this, to David I. He knew that, in 1238, Alexander II had promised that Bruce 'the Competitor' would be the next king. (This was before the birth of Alexander's son, who became Alexander III.) Also, Edward I had promised Bruce's father that *he* would rule Scotland if King John was deposed.

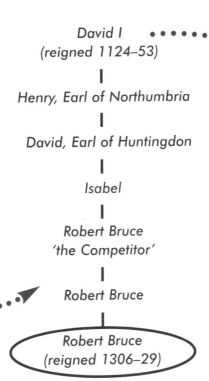

David I
(reigned 1124–53)

|

Henry, Earl of Northumbria

|

David, Earl of Huntingdon

|

Isabel

|

Robert Bruce
'the Competitor'

|

Robert Bruce

|

Robert Bruce
(reigned 1306–29)

▲ This 12th-century illustration shows David I with his grandson, Malcolm IV. Notice their crowns, sceptre and orb, all part of the monarch's regalia.

The war continues

In 1298, after the defeat of Wallace and the Scots at Falkirk, Robert Bruce and John Comyn became Guardians. The Bruces and the Comyns were still bitter rivals and this hindered the struggle for independence.

Edward I and his son Edward, Prince of Wales, harried the Scots every year. Then they tried to win over the Scots people by allowing them their own laws, and returning confiscated lands if they paid a fine. But the brutal treatment of Wallace in 1305 destroyed any goodwill that Edward may have gained.

The murder of Comyn

Bruce pretended still to be loyal to Edward I, so that his lands would not be forfeited. In

1305 he and John Comyn signed a pledge that Comyn would get all Bruce's lands for helping Bruce to become king. Then Bruce heard that Comyn had told Edward I of this agreement. He arranged to meet Comyn in Greyfriars' Church in Dumfries on 10 February 1306. The men quarrelled, daggers were drawn and Bruce stabbed Comyn, who died in front of the altar.

▶ *Bruce and Comyn fight in front of the altar. Afterwards, Bruce confessed his crime to the Bishop of Glasgow and the powerful Scottish Church supported him as king.*

King Robert I

The Comyns wanted revenge and Bruce could not rely on Edward I for protection. He decided that his best hope was to make himself king. On 25 March 1306 he was hastily crowned at Scone. There was no Stone of Destiny (see page 9) and Edward I had plundered the crown and other regalia. Traditionally, monarchs were crowned at Scone by the Earl of Fife, but Edward I would not allow the Earl to leave England. The Earl's sister, Isabel, rode to Scone, and two days later, in a second coronation, she placed a circlet of gold on Bruce's head.

A real king?

Some people thought that, without a traditional coronation, Bruce was not really a king. Copy and complete these sentences explaining people's feelings.

■ Robert Bruce is not the real king of Scotland because...

■ I believe Robert Bruce is the real king of Scotland because...

◀ *This waxwork at Edinburgh Castle shows Isabel, Countess of Buchan, crowning Bruce on Palm Sunday, 1306.*

Setbacks and successes

Although Bruce was now king, he was still in danger. By murdering John Comyn, he had turned many families against him. Edward I announced that anyone involved in Bruce's rebellion would be executed without trial.

Methven

In June 1306 Bruce raised an army of 4,500 men and marched to Perth, which was held for the English by the Earl of Pembroke. Bruce called for the Earl's forces to fight or surrender. The Earl said that he would fight tomorrow, but at dusk that day he launched a surprise attack on Bruce's men in their camp at Methven. Bruce and a few supporters escaped on horseback.

Dalrigh

Followers of Comyn attacked the Scottish king and his men at Dalrigh. Bruce's wife, daughter and other noblewomen fled northwards, but were captured by English soldiers and imprisoned in England. Bruce ordered his men to retreat, as so many had been wounded or killed, and he took refuge with them on Rathlin Island, off the coast

▲ Bruce faced many dangers and disappointments after he was crowned, sometimes sleeping on the hillsides or hiding in caves, like these at Drumadoon Point on the island of Arran.

of Ireland. Early in 1307 he returned to Scotland and retook Turnberry Castle, his possible birthplace, from the English.

New tactics

As his men were always far outnumbered, Bruce was unlikely to defeat his enemies in pitched battles and so he adopted the tactics of guerrilla warfare. He took to the hills and frequently moved his headquarters, to outsmart his enemies. He could choose when and where to attack, using the layout of the land to his advantage. Soft ground was difficult for cavalry and narrow passes enabled a few men to drive back a much larger force. Many attacks took place at night, as the element of surprise was very important.

As Bruce's success increased, more Scots joined his army, believing that he could now lead them to independence. Edward I died on 11 July 1307. His son, Edward II, had less enthusiasm for war. This gave the Scots time to strengthen their position. Gradually Bruce destroyed the Comyns and retook most of the Scottish castles.

▼ On 14 March 1314, Bruce's nephew and his men climbed the north face of the rock and recaptured Edinburgh Castle. Bruce ordered that the castle be destroyed so that it could not provide a stronghold for the English army again.

▼ *In May 1307, Bruce's men awaited the English army at Loudon Hill. The land below was about 500 metres wide and bordered by marsh. Bruce cut trenches in the approach to the hill, to create a narrow path. This meant that with only 600 men, he was able to repel 3,000 Englishmen.*

War tactics

Imagine you are either Robert Bruce or a commander of the English army. Write a speech explaining to your men what military tactics you will use to defeat the enemy. Remember to say what tactics the enemy will use.

Bannockburn

Stirling Castle guarded the route between the north and south of Scotland. The castle was held by the English and besieged by the Scots. In 1313 the commander of the English troops at Stirling agreed to surrender if English reinforcements had not arrived by midsummer 1314.

Preparing for battle

Bruce realised that his army would have to fight a pitched battle and so he spent the next year training his men. They would fight in formations called schiltrons, and these would move forwards like a battering ram.

Edward II's army numbered 2,500 cavalry, 3,000 archers and 15,000 infantry. Edward intended not just to reinforce the defence of Stirling Castle, but to destroy the Scottish army once and for all. Bruce had only about 5,000 fully trained men.

Bruce chose the site for the battle, making use of slopes, burns – including the Bannock Burn – and boggy land. His army dug pits and camouflaged them with broken branches and twigs, to hinder an English cavalry charge.

▲ *Imagine what it was like standing shoulder to shoulder in a schiltron, with spears pointing at the charging enemy. Wallace also used schiltrons at the Battle of Stirling Bridge.*

23 June 1314

On the eve of the battle Bruce positioned his men on a rise where they could see the English advance. An English knight, Sir Henry de Bohun, recognised Bruce and charged at him. Bruce, on a smaller, more agile pony, swerved and brought his battle-axe crashing down, killing Bohun. The Scottish forces eagerly charged down the hill, but Bruce called them back. The English army was stunned.

24 June 1314

Early in the morning three divisions of schiltrons, about 2,500 men, advanced towards the English army. The English cavalry charged. Horses stumbled into the camouflaged pits and unseated their riders, who were trampled underfoot or impaled on the Scottish spears. There was close, bloody, hand-to-hand fighting. The English archers dared not fire, for fear of hitting their own men, and the infantry could not advance in the chaos. Scottish reinforcements stampeded down the hill, scattering the English army. Edward II was defeated.

After the battle

Edward escaped, leaving behind the royal treasure and the Great Seal of England. The Scots took many prisoners, but they were treated well. Bruce insisted that the nobles were cared for as guests until their ransoms were paid. He also made sure that the English dead were buried with respect.

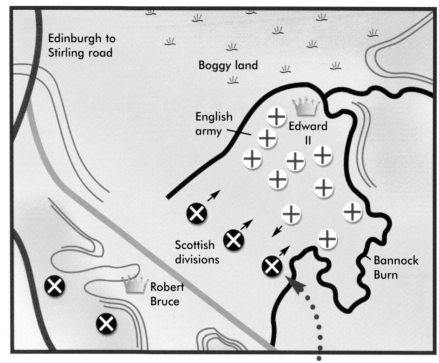

▲ The Bannock Burn protected this division of schiltrons from English attack. The battle became known as the Battle of Bannockburn.

▶ The head of a battle axe. Other weapons used at Bannockburn included spears, maces and longbows.

Be a war correspondent

Tape-record an account of the battle from the point of view of an English or a Scottish soldier. These questions will get you started:

- Why did you fight at Bannockburn?
- What weapons did you have?
- What weapons did the enemy have?
- Was the enemy well organised?
- What was the most frightening part of the battle?

After Bannockburn

Victory at the Battle of Bannockburn was important for the Scots but did not end the war. For Scotland, peace with England would mean security and the chance to trade more with England and other countries. But Edward II stubbornly refused Bruce's offer of peace.

Raids into England

The Scots raided undefended towns in the north of England, demanding money in return for leaving them undamaged. Crops were destroyed and sheep and cattle from English farms were driven north to Scotland.

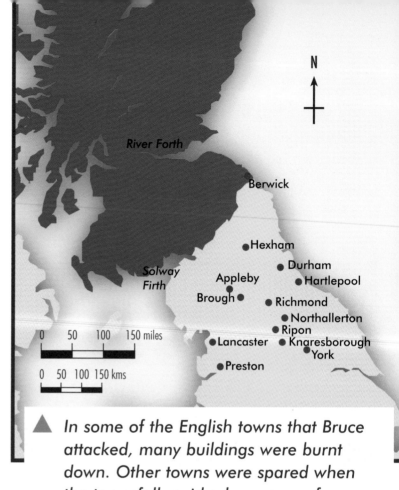

▲ In some of the English towns that Bruce attacked, many buildings were burnt down. Other towns were spared when the townsfolk paid a large sum of money.

> Now... the Scottish army invaded England and marched into Durham. James Douglas and the Steward of Scotland went forward plundering the country in all directions, one of them raiding towards Hartlepool and the other towards Richmond. The people of Richmond, having no defender, bought off the invaders with a great sum of money.

▲ This extract from an English chronicle shows how the Scottish raids were recorded at the time. How would reports in Scottish chronicles have been different?

The Earl of Lancaster

Edward II suspected that the Earl of Lancaster, an English noble, was no longer loyal to him, because the Scots never raided the Earl's land. With a friend, role-play a question and answer session where Edward enquires into the Earl's loyalty.

In 1319 Bruce devised a plan to kidnap and ransom the English queen at York while Edward II was laying siege to Berwick. The plot was discovered, but it made the English generals lift the siege of Berwick and march south to protect their own people. Edward II finally agreed to a two-year truce.

Edward attacks again

No sooner had the truce ended, in 1322, than Edward raised a huge army and marched up the east coast, determined to wipe out his enemy. Bruce made all Scots people living south of the River Forth move north with their animals, burning buildings and crops as they went. This meant that there was no food or shelter for Edward's army and, in September, hunger forced them to retreat.

The Battle of Old Byland

Bruce continued to harry the north of England. In October 1322 he marched his men from the Solway to Northallerton, knowing that Edward II was at nearby Rievaulx Abbey.

Their path was blocked by an English army, who had the higher ground and commanded the narrow pass to the top of the moor. The Scots fought bravely, but progress was slow until Bruce sent his Highland reservists to scramble up a steep slope, hidden from the English, and charge down from the top. Taken by surprise, the English fled. Bruce's army marched on to try to capture Edward, but the king had heard of the threat and escaped.

Why do you think some people said that this battle, called the Battle of Old Byland, was more important for the Scots than the Battle of Bannockburn?

Edward II and Queen Isabella were staying at Rievaulx Abbey when the English army was surprisingly defeated at the Battle of Old Byland. The king and queen fled but, once again, left behind the king's treasure, including the Great Seal of England. When Edward had left the Seal behind after Bannockburn, Bruce had generously returned it.

The Declaration of Arbroath

The Church and its leader, the Pope, were very influential in medieval times. What the Pope said was taken very seriously.

A problem for Bruce was that the Pope had excommunicated him, partly for his terrible crime of killing John Comyn in a church. The excommunication meant that Bruce was banned from any church services and Christians must have no contact with him. Therefore Christians in other countries, such as France, were not able to support him. The Pope also refused to address Bruce as king.

The Scots write to the Pope

In 1320 Bernard de Linton, Abbot of Arbroath, wrote to the Pope on behalf of many Scottish nobles. They thought that if the Pope could be persuaded to accept Bruce as king, other monarchs, including Edward II, would do the same.

The Abbot wrote that Scotland had been a free and independent nation for centuries, until Edward I attacked its people, murdering and plundering as he went. He described how 'our most valiant Prince and King, Lord Robert'

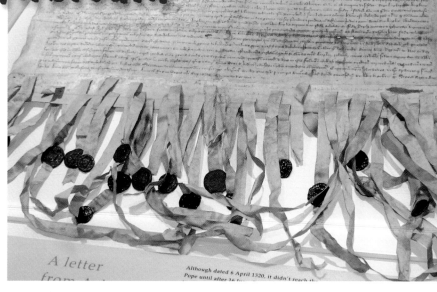

A letter
from A...

Although dated 6 April 1320, it didn't reach the
Pope until after 16 J...

▲ The long document written to the Pope in Latin by the Abbot of Arbroath is called the Declaration of Arbroath. The nobles signed and attached their seals to it on 6 April 1320. It was not signed by any churchmen or by Bruce, in case that annoyed the Pope.

fought to free Scotland, but the English king would not recognise Scotland's independence.

Pope John XXII was keen that there should be a crusade to the Holy Land. So Bernard wrote that the English preferred to fight an easy war against the weaker Scots than to go on a crusade. He also hinted that the Pope would be responsible for more bloodshed if war continued between England and Scotland.

A famous part of the Declaration

Yet if [our king] should give up what he has begun, and agree to make us or our kingdom subject to the King of England or the English, we should exert ourselves at once to drive him out as our enemy and a subverter of his own rights and ours, and make some other man who was well able to defend us our King; for, as long as but a hundred of us remain alive, never will we on any conditions be brought under English rule.

▲ What does this part of the Declaration say the Scottish people can do, if their king surrenders to English rule?

The Pope's reaction

The Pope wrote to Edward II almost immediately, telling him to make peace with the Scots, but this did not happen. In 1324 the Pope finally realised that, to bring peace between England and Scotland, he must address Robert Bruce as king. The Pope wrote to Edward II: 'You will know that my Bull… will never be received in Scotland if I address it under any appellation but that of king.'

Edward II was not pleased, but had to agree to discuss a formal peace treaty between England and Scotland.

The character of Bruce

In this book you have read lots of information about Robert Bruce. Here are some sentences which tell you what sort of man he was. Find information in this book or elsewhere that supports these statements.

- Bruce was a great leader.
- He had a temper.
- He could be generous and kind.
- He could be violent.
- He was a popular king.

Now think of some more sentences to describe his character.

▼ One side of Bruce's royal seal shows him on the throne; the other shows him armed for battle. In medieval Scotland, kingship meant being both a just ruler and a protecting, fearless warrior.

The end of a reign

In 1327 Edward II was forced to abdicate in favour of his son, Edward III. The following year the Treaty of Edinburgh/Northampton was signed. The treaty stated that Edward III recognised Scotland as an independent kingdom.

A last request

By 1329 Bruce was 54 years old and in poor health. He may have suffered from leprosy, a serious skin disease. In the early summer he summoned his most loyal companions. He explained to them that he had taken an oath that, when Scotland was peaceful and safe, he would go on a crusade. Now he realised that he would not be able to go and so he asked that, after his death, one of his companions should take his heart and carry it on a crusade. They discussed who should have the honour and chose Sir James Douglas, one of the bravest of Bruce's knights.

On 7 June 1329 King Robert I died at Cardross. His heart was removed and put in a small casket. His body was buried at Dunfermline Abbey, among the earlier kings of Scotland.

▲ *In medieval times soldiers from many countries went to fight in crusades, to protect holy places in the Middle East.*

King Robert's heart

Sir James Douglas set sail from Berwick for the Holy Land in early 1330. He stayed for some time in Spain and, while he was there, that part of the country was attacked. On 25 August 1330, Douglas became involved in the fight between Spanish and Arab soldiers.

Timeline

Draw up an illustrated timeline of the main events in Bruce's life.

Leaping to his horse, Douglas charged at the Arabs, carrying Bruce's heart in a silver and enamel casket around his neck. Some people say that he hurled the casket into the midst of the enemy, before he was killed.

Douglas's bones were returned to Scotland, and the casket was rescued and buried at Melrose Abbey.

In 1996, archaeologists excavating at Melrose Abbey unearthed a lead casket. Inside it they found a smaller, cone-shaped casket, marked with these words: 'The enclosed leaden casket containing a heart was found beneath Chapter House floor, March 1921, by His Majesty's Office of Works.' The casket was reburied in 1998, without being reopened. Do you think we could know for certain whether the heart was Robert Bruce's?

▼ *Scientists drilled a small hole in the lead casket found in 1996 and looked inside with a fibre-optic cable. They could see a smaller casket inside and carefully took it out.*

▲ *Melrose Abbey was damaged by Edward II's army in 1322. Bruce gave money to help the monks to restore it.*

▶ *This stone marks the spot where the casket was reburied in 1998.*

How do we know?

Documentary evidence

Eyewitness accounts of events are most reliable if they are written down immediately, but at the time of Bruce and Wallace only churchmen, some noblemen and a very few noblewomen could read and write. Why do you think there are few eyewitness accounts of the events in this book?

Chronicles are records of events, often written by churchmen. Several chronicles, some by Englishmen and some by Scotsmen, tell about the exploits of Bruce. Why do you think the writers often interpret the events differently?

Only important people would write letters. If these survive, they can give lots of information about the past. Some letters have been used as sources of information for this book.

Often people would recount adventures to a scribe. After Bruce's death, John Barbour (1320?-95) wrote an exciting long poem, 'The Brus', describing the struggle for independence. Barbour was not an eyewitness to any of the

A! Fredome is a noble thing!
Fredome mays man to haiff liking;
Fredome all solace to man giffis,
He levys at ese that frely levys!
A noble hart may haiff nane ese,
Na ellys nocht that may him plese,
Gyff fredome fail; for fre liking
Is yarnyt our all othir thing.

Ah! Freedom is a noble thing!
Freedom makes a man content
Freedom all solace to man gives
He lives at ease that freely lives.
A noble heart may have no ease
Nor anything else that may him please
If Freedom fail, for freedom of choice
Is desired above all else.

▲ This is a verse from 'The Brus' by John Barbour, with a modern translation.

◀ The Stone of Destiny, stolen by Edward I in 1296, was returned to Scotland in 1996 and is now kept at Edinburgh Castle.

events, but it is possible that eyewitnesses recounted the tales to him. 'The Brus' gives historians a great deal of information about the times, so it is a very important piece of literature.

A minstrel known as Blind Harry lived between about 1440 and 1492. He wrote a long poem about William Wallace. Do you think this poem is likely to be as accurate as Barbour's? Why?

Bruce and the spider

Read the story of Bruce and the spider at http://www.longlong timeago.com/llta_history_bruce.html. This story first appeared in print in the 1820s. Do you think it is fact or myth? Why?

What did people look like?

There are no contemporary pictures of Robert Bruce, but artefacts and remains give some information. In 1818 a skeleton, wrapped in the remains of fine, gold cloth, was found at Dunfermline Abbey. There was evidence that the heart had been cut out. People think this was probably Bruce. The size of the skeleton (5' 11" tall) can tell us about his height and build, and a cast was made of his skull. Nowadays skilled artists can build up a clay likeness from a skull. The face of the statue of Bruce at Bannockburn (right) was modelled in this way.

Using clay placed over a plaster cast of a person's skull, it is possible to build a picture of how the person looked.

Think about what you have learned about Robert Bruce, William Wallace and the first War of Independence. What sources have provided the information?

Glossary

abbot the person in charge of an abbey.

abdicate to resign as king.

altar a special table in a church, used in religious ceremonies.

Anglo-Normans people whose ancestors first came to England from Normandy with William the Conqueror in 1066.

appellation an old-fashioned word for 'name'.

archaeologist someone who finds out about the past by looking at what people leave behind (e.g. buildings, tools, bones).

artefacts man-made objects.

auditors people like a jury who listened to the evidence given when Bruce 'the Competitor' and John Balliol both claimed the throne.

baron a less important nobleman than an earl or a duke.

battering ram a piece of equipment, like a tree trunk, used to knock things down by hitting them.

besieged surrounded by enemy soldiers so that no food or other supplies can get in.

betray to give information about someone (usually a friend) to their enemies.

bishop an important churchman.

Bull an instruction from the Pope.

cavalry soldiers on horseback, making part of an army.

chronicle a record of events, often in story form.

confiscate to take something away, as a punishment.

contender someone who fights or competes to win something.

continent a large area of land. 'The Continent' often means the rest of Europe.

coronation a ceremony to crown a king or queen.

council a group that meets to discuss and make decisions about important matters, often advising a monarch.

crusade a holy war in which medieval soldiers fought to protect holy places.

depose to overthrow.

earl a nobleman more important than a baron.

excommunicate to ban someone from church services; a punishment from the Pope.

eyewitness account a description of an event by someone who saw it.

feudal overlord an important person who leases land to a less important tenant (vassal). In exchange the tenant (vassal) must do military service for his overlord.

forfeited lost or given up as a penalty for doing something wrong.

Great Offices of State important posts given by the king, including Chancellor, Chamberlain, Constable and Justiciars.

Guardians people who ruled Scotland in the name of a monarch who was too young to rule or was living overseas.

guerrilla warfare attacks on an enemy by small groups of soldiers, often relying on surprise.

harry	to torment, destroy or plunder.	**regalia**	the crown, orb and sceptre etc, which are symbols of monarchy.
heir	a person who will inherit goods or a title when the present holder dies.	**reinforcements**	extra soldiers, who provide more fighting power later in a battle.
Holy Land	land in the Middle East where Jesus lived.	**repel**	to drive back.
impaled	pierced with a sharp object.	**reservists**	soldiers who are not part of the main army, perhaps because they are older or not well enough trained or armed. They are used as reinforcements.
infantry	foot soldiers in an army.		
knight	a man who fought on horseback for his feudal overlord in exchange for land.		
lease	to rent out.	**revoke**	to reject parts or all of a treaty.
military	to do with warfare.	**schiltron**	a detachment of soldiers, armed with spears, standing shoulder to shoulder.
minstrel	an entertainer who wrote and sang poems, often playing a lute.	**scribe**	someone who writes down an account told by another person.
monarch	a king or queen.	**seal**	an engraved piece of stone or metal which was pressed on wax attached to documents to show they were genuine.
oath	a promise sworn on the Bible.		
outlaw	a person who is not given the protection of the law because they are a criminal or bandit.		
parliament	a meeting of people to make decisions and pass laws for their country.	**siege**	surrounding a town or castle and cutting off its supplies in an attempt to force the people inside to surrender.
patriot	someone very loyal to their country.	**slaughtered**	murdered or massacred in a violent way.
pay homage	to swear an oath to be loyal to a feudal superior.	**stampede**	to rush in a crowd in the same direction.
pitched battle	a battle between two armies, fought on ground chosen by one army.	**tactics**	plans or scheme.
pledge	a promise.	**treason**	disloyalty to or betrayal of a monarch or country.
plunder	to steal, rob or loot.	**treaty**	a written agreement, usually between two countries.
Pope	the head of the whole Christian church at the time of Robert Bruce.	**trenches**	ditches.
raid	to attack suddenly.	**truce**	a cease fire.
ransom	money paid to buy freedom for a prisoner held by the enemy.	**valiant**	brave, heroic or fearless.

For teachers and parents

This book is designed to develop children's historical knowledge, understanding and skills, with a Scottish focus within the medieval period. Throughout the book and in the associated activities children are encouraged to consider the chronology of events and the nature of the available historical evidence. The activities are designed to act as a starting point for further research, and in every case the children should plan their work carefully, select from the information available in this book and elsewhere, and present their findings appropriately.

While the activities are designed principally to develop history skills, they often make links with other curriculum subjects, and children are encouraged to use ICT where appropriate, particularly for further research and presentation. The book also gives opportunities for developing responsible attitudes to others.

SUGGESTED FURTHER ACTIVITIES

Pages 4 - 5 The two kingdoms
Although Scotland and England co-existed in relative peace, there were frequent skirmishes along the border and parts of this land were at one time in Scotland and later in England. Most of the borderlands were rough grazing and of little financial value, but the town of Berwick was different. It had important trade links with wool merchants in Flanders.

Children could find out how the ordinary people lived, what their homes were like, what they ate and what clothes they wore. They could make model houses. They could go on to find out about the main burghs (e.g. Perth, Aberdeen, Edinburgh and Glasgow); where and why they developed and what links they had with other countries.

Pages 6 - 7 A kingdom without a monarch
Alexander III's daughter, Margaret, was betrothed to Erik of Norway as part of the Treaty of Perth in 1266. Under the terms of this treaty the Isle of Man and the Hebrides were restored to Scotland. Norway still ruled over the Orkneys and Shetlands.

Children could role-play the scene of Alexander III's courtiers trying to persuade him not to ride to his queen on the night he fell to his death.

Pages 8 - 9 The new king of Scotland
Children could find out who the main claimants to the throne of Scotland were from:
http://en.wikipedia.org/wiki/Competitors_for_the_Crown_of_Scotland.
They could create simple family trees for some of these people.

Speeches could be written for Robert 'the Competitor' and John Balliol, in which the children explain why each claimant should succeed.

Pages 10 - 11 William Wallace
A sword reputed to have been owned and used by Wallace is on display at the Wallace monument in Stirling. Children could use the information at http://www.stirling.gov.uk/index/stirling/wallace/wallace_sword.htm to make a life-size replica of the sword, from card, balsa or jelutong, and see how difficult it would have been to wield.

Using contours on maps for guidance, children could make a 3D model of the site of the Battle of Stirling Bridge.

Children could work in groups to find out the details of the Battle of Falkirk and make a report to the rest of the class.

There are similarities between Wallace and Bruce, including their guerrilla tactics and use of schiltrons. Children could begin to draw up a table of similarities and differences, adding to it as they discover more.

Pages 12 - 13 The nobles of Scotland
As the principal noblemen held land in both kingdoms, there was no real sense of national identity as we understand it today. Behaviour was often influenced by personal interest and noblemen were likely to support the side that appeared to be winning. This was not usually considered treacherous.

Children could plan and carry out research, using the Internet, to find details about some of the other main characters and their roles in the Wars of Independence: for example, Sir Thomas Randolph, Sir James Douglas, Walter Stewart, Edward and Nigel Bruce.

In 1296 Edward I insisted that all landholders and other important people should swear allegiance to him and attach their seals to a document showing that they recognised Edward as their only king. This document was called the Ragman Roll. Children could look for the names of the main characters at http://www.rampantscotland.com/ragman/blragman_a.htm.

Pages 14 - 15 Robert Bruce becomes king
Greyfriars' Church in Dumfries had been endowed by John Balliol's mother. The church is no longer standing.

Children could find out more details about John Comyn and give some reasons why Bruce needed the support of the Comyns to become king. They could explain the short-term and longer-term effects for Bruce of Comyn's death.

Coronations are full of ritual and tradition, which help to create a sense of continuity. Children could write about traditions in their own families (e.g. special meals or a Christmas Day timetable), schools, or nationally, and find out how the traditions started or evolved.

Pages 16 - 17 Setbacks and successes

The queen (Bruce's second wife, Elizabeth de Burgh), her step-daughter Marjorie and several female companions tried to escape to the Orkneys. Bruce's sister was the dowager queen of Norway, so help would be forthcoming. However, the ladies were captured and some of them were held in unspeakable conditions, kept like animals in cages on public view. The queen was kept in almost solitary confinement for many years.

After the Battle of Dalrigh, Bruce and his men spent much time in the hills. The children could consider techniques needed for survival, listing needs and possible sources.

Pages 18 - 19 Bannockburn

Wallace used a schiltron formation with soldiers facing outwards in all directions, providing defence on all sides. Bruce used the formation like a battering ram, to attack, as the rear and sides of the schiltron were protected in other ways. As a class, children could form themselves into the two different schiltron formations used by Wallace and Bruce and see how much more difficult it is to move one formation than the other.

Children could find out about the different weapons used at the battle, then draw pictures and annotate them.

Bruce treated all prisoners with dignity and compassion. Some were returned without ransom, others were kept in comfortable surroundings until their ransom was paid. Children could compare Bruce's treatment of prisoners with what they know about the way the English king and his men behaved towards captives, for example the queen's companions and William Wallace.

Pages 20 - 21 After Bannockburn

Each clan had its own war cry, which was used to identify members of the same family in times of confusion. The Douglases shouted 'Douglas, Douglas!' and the Macfarlanes' cry was 'Loch Sloy!' Children could use the Internet to research clan war cries, or make up some appropriate ones of their own.

The Battle of Old Byland is seen as an important victory for Robert Bruce because it took place in England.

Pages 22 - 23 The Declaration of Arbroath

The Declaration of Arbroath can be found at: http://www.geo.ed.ac.uk/home/Scotland/arbroath.htm. With adult help, children could read the Declaration in full and identify the key points made by Bernard de Linton. They could write the Declaration in modern-day language.

Children could use clay to make their own seals, and then impress them on wet clay or Plasticine. The design should reflect their names or something about their lives.

Older children could write a speech explaining the importance of freedom in today's world.

Pages 24 - 25 The end of a reign

The casket containing Bruce's heart was opened in 1921 and reburied. It was not reopened in 1996. Children could debate whether they think the casket should have been reopened. What might have been learnt? What might new techniques in forensic medicine have told us? What would have been the implications if investigations had revealed something that people didn't want to know?

Some people say that Bruce was Scotland's greatest king. Although the children have insufficient knowledge to judge, they could suggest qualities that might support this claim.

Pages 26 - 27 How do we know?

Play 'Chinese whispers', which illustrates how facts become distorted as they are passed on by word of mouth.

Children could find out biographical details about Andrew Wyntoun, who wrote the 'Orygynal Cronykil of Scotland', and John Barbour, who wrote 'The Brus'. They could comment on any possible bias in the writings of Wyntoun and Barbour, compared with the Chronicles of Lanercost, which were written by English monks. These can be found at: http://www.deremilitari.org/RESOURCES/SOURCES/lanercost.htm.

Read a translation of parts of Barbour's poem. The children could then compose their own poem about an event in Bruce's life. Some might relish the challenge of writing rhyming octosyllabic lines, like Barbour.

The Stone of Destiny taken by Edward I (see page 9) does not match descriptions of it in early Scottish literature. The children could debate the authenticity of the stone kept in Edinburgh Castle. If it is not the original, what might have happened to the real one and why?

INTERNET RESOURCES

There are numerous websites with information about Robert Bruce and William Wallace. Not all of them are accurate and children should be encouraged to question their reliability.

http://www.heritage.me.uk/people/bruce.htm

http://web.channel4.com/learning/main/netnotes/sectionid100663958.htm

http://www.bbc.co.uk/history/scottishhistory/independence/index.shtml

http://en.wikipedia.org/wiki/Wars_of_Scottish_Independence

http://en.wikipedia.org/wiki/Robert_I_of_Scotland

http://www.royal.gov.uk/output/Page5.asp (provides biographical information about all Scottish and English monarchs)

http://www.scotland.gov.uk/News/News-Extras/208 (from the National Archives, the Treaty of Edinburgh/Northampton)

http://www.castlesontheweb.com

http://www.scran.ac.uk/ (Scran online learning resource service with free access for Scottish schools. On this site there are numerous high-quality pictorial resources, including original documents.)

Index